ASTON VILLA
FOOTBALL CLUB

The Official Annual 2019

Compiled by Rob Bishop and ArenaOne

Special thanks to Gayner Monkton

A Grange Publication

© 2018. Published by Grange Communications Ltd., Edinburgh, under licence from Aston Villa Football Club. Printed in the EU.

Photographs © [Neville Williams / Getty Images]

ISBN: 978-1-912595-01-3

CLUB HONOURS

EUROPEAN CUP WINNERS:
1981-82

QUARTER-FINALISTS:
1982-83

EUROPEAN SUPER CUP WINNERS:
1982-83

WORLD CLUBS CHAMPIONSHIP RUNNERS-UP:
1982

INTERTOTO CUP WINNERS:
2001

FOOTBALL LEAGUE CHAMPIONS:
1893-94, 1895-96, 1896-97, 1898-99, 1899-1900, 1909-10, 1980-81

RUNNERS-UP:
1888-89, 1902-03, 1907-08, 1910-11, 1912-13, 1913-14, 1930-31, 1932-33, 1989-90

PREMIER LEAGUE RUNNERS-UP:
1992-93

DIVISION TWO CHAMPIONS:
1937-38, 1959-60

DIVISION THREE CHAMPIONS:
1971-72

FA CUP WINNERS:
1887, 1895, 1897, 1905, 1913, 1920, 1957

RUNNERS-UP:
1892, 1924, 2000, 2015

LEAGUE CUP WINNERS:
1961, 1975, 1977, 1994, 1996

RUNNERS-UP:
1963, 1971, 2010

FA YOUTH CUP WINNERS:
1972, 1980, 2002

RUNNERS-UP:
2004, 2010

Contents

3.	Credits
4.	Honours
5.	Contents
6.	New Signings
7.	New Signings
8.	New Signings
9.	New Signings
10.	New Signings
11.	Poster
12.	First Goals Club
13.	First Goals Club
14.	Let's go to the Movies
15.	A Dresden Double
16.	2018/19 Squad
17.	2018/19 Squad
18.	2018/19 Squad
19.	2018/19 Squad
20.	2018/19 Squad
21.	2018/19 Squad
22.	Do you know James Chester?
23.	Poster
24.	Poster
25.	2017/18 Season Reveiw
26.	2017/18 Season Reveiw
27.	2017/18 Season Reveiw
28.	2017/18 Season Reveiw
29.	2017/18 Season Reveiw
30.	2017/18 Season Reveiw
31.	2017/18 Season Reveiw
32.	2017/18 Season Reveiw
33.	2017/18 Season Reveiw
34.	2017/18 Season Reveiw
35.	2017/18 Season Reveiw
36.	Conor's 11
37.	Conor's 11
38.	Spot the Difference
39.	Players and Places
40.	10 Years of Home Kits
41.	10 Years of Home Kits
42.	Poster
43.	Would you believe it?
44.	Poster
45.	Getting Shirty
46.	Fit for a Prince
47.	The Scottish Cafu
48.	Poster
49.	It's Villa Park - But not as we know it
50.	The Aston Academy
51.	The Aston Academy
52.	Poster
53.	That's My Home
54.	Cub Membership
55.	Cub Membership
56.	Poster
57.	The Numbers Game
58.	Vital Villa Park
59.	Poster
60.	Answers
61.	Answers
62.	Can you spot Hercules?
63.	Can you spot Hercules?

TAKE A SEAT!

Footballers don't always need to play for a club to know it's the right place for them.

John McGinn decided Villa was the club for him once he had been shown around our famous stadium.

"As soon as I saw Villa Park I had a gut feeling about the place," he said. "When I sat in the stand at Villa Park I could picture myself playing here. It just felt right.

"I'm excited to be part of the vision the club have – this is a Premier League club and we are going to work as hard as possible to get there."

The Scotland international agreed his move from Hibernian just before the transfer window closed and by coming to England he has followed in the footsteps of his older brothers, who are both also professional footballers.

Although they are now both at St Mirren, Stephen played for Watford between 2010 and 2013, while Paul had a season with Chesterfield.

"Mum and dad are proud to have three of us playing football," he said. "And let's not forget my twin sister Katie, who has been very supportive."

"I'm excited to be part of the vision the club have."

John describes himself as a player who always gives 100 per cent and works hard even when he is not at his best. "I want to bring a lot of energy to Villa's midfield," he said.

NEW SIGNING
JOHN McGINN

Their positions couldn't be more different, but Ørjan Nyland will have no complaints if he can be as productive as the last Norwegian to play for Villa.

Striker John Carew's job was to score goals, while Ørjan's is to make saves. But the Norway international keeper is determined to enjoy his time with Villa as much as the man supporters used to serenade with the words: "He's gonna score one or two."

"John Carew had a lot of success here and that's something I want, too," said Ørjan. "Interest in Aston Villa was big in Norway when John played for the club and I watched a lot of Villa games on TV when I was growing up.

"Now I want to be part of the club's history. Hopefully I can play a part in getting them back to where they belong. This club belongs in the Premier League, and they almost clinched promotion last season."

Ørjan spent most of his early career in his homeland, first with Hodd and then Molde, before joining Bundesliga club Ingolstadt 04 in 2015 and spending the past three seasons in Germany.

Although he speaks English, Ørjan is often able to converse in his native tongue in the dressing room – thanks to Icelandic midfielder Birkir Bjarnason.

The two players have known each other for a while and have the same agent – and Birkir can speak Norwegian!

HE'S GONNA SAVE ONE OR TWO!

NEW SIGNING
ØRJAN NYLAND

Tammy's target...
Young striker wants plenty of goals

Tammy Abraham became Villa's seventh signing when he arrived on the loan transfer deadline day at the end of August.

And he admits his decision was influenced by a couple of players who have already made a big impact in claret-and-blue shirt.

"Jack Grealish was messaging me every day, urging me to come here," said the highly-rated Chelsea striker. "It's nice to have someone you know when you come to a new club.

"And I'm looking forward to a partnership with Jonathan Kodjia. I played alongside him for Bristol City a couple of time and he provided the assist for my first professional goal."

That was early in the 2016-17 season when Tammy – real name Kevin Bakumo-Abraham – was on loan to Bristol City, and he went on to score over 20 goals for the Ashton Gate club.

After spending last season on loan to Swansea City, Tammy was told he would be needed back at Stamford Bridge, and he was involved in the pre-season Community Shield game against Manchester City at Wembley.

But when it became evident that his chances of playing regularly in the Premier League would be limited, he opted to a loan move to Villa Park.

"I want to make a name for myself," he said. "I missed Villa's first few games of the season, but I want to score as many goals as possible and hopefully help the team to promotion."

When he was making his decision, Tammy also received some advice from John Terry, the former Chelsea and England star, who was Villa's captain last season.

"John was one of the first people to call me," he said. "He told me that this is a great club."

NEW LOANEE
TAMMY ABRAHAM

RAIN MAN!
English weather no problem for Andre

Overseas players who come to this country often have to acclimatise to the English weather – but that's no problem for Andre Moreira.

The 22-year-old goalkeeper, who joined Villa on a season-long loan from Atletico Madrid, was born in the town of Ribeirao in northern Portugal, where temperatures are nowhere near as hot as in the south.

"English weather is just like winter in Portugal," he said. "I'm from the north, where it's not so hot. It's rainy and windy in the winter, so I am used to those conditions."

Andre started his career with his hometown club and was so impressive for Portugal under-19s at the 2014 European Championships that he was signed on a six-year contract by Spanish giants Atletico.

He has spent the past four seasons on loan to Portuguese clubs and relished the chance of playing in England for the first time.

"It's such a big opportunity to join a great club like this," he said. "The training facilities are great, and the players tried to make me feel at home as soon as I arrived."

Zzzzzzzzzzzzzzzz!
IT'S A SLEEPY START FOR AXEL

A good night's sleep is essential to a footballer's performance. But Axel Tuanzebe got precious little shut-eye when he became a Villa player for the second time in August.

On the Sunday evening, he went on as a 78th-minute substitute for Manchester United in their final pre-season friendly against Bayern Munich in Germany. Little more than 12 hours later, he was completing a season-long loan agreement with Villa.

"United flew back after the game and I didn't get home until around 5am," he said. "I certainly didn't get very much sleep!

"But it was a great experience to play at the Allianz Arena – and great to be back at Villa Park the following morning."

Axel first joined Villa on loan in January but injury problems restricted him to just five appearances during the second half of last season. Now he is hoping the claret-and-blue faithful will see the best of him.

"Coming in at the start of the season means you are involved from the get-go," he said. "Last season, things were already in place here and it was hard to break through."

Anwar the film star

If you want an insight into what goes on behind the scenes when a new player joins a football club, check out the YouTube video of Anwar El Ghazi's arrival at Villa Park.

The fascinating film shows Anwar being greeted at Birmingham Airport before being driven to Villa Park for a look at the home dressing room and an atmospheric late-night photo on the pitch.

The following day, the film crew captured the Dutch winger being taken to the club's training ground and undergoing the medical checks which are part and parcel of every signing.

Anwar, on loan from French club Lille, is also interviewed in the taxi, and can't hide his delight at becoming a Villa player.

He admits that he had "goosebumps" when he saw the stadium – and was so thrilled that he took photos on his phone and sent them to his family.

A few days later, he made an immediate impact, providing a superb cross from which Ahmed Elmohamady headed Villa's goal against Reading.

Wow, what a stadium!

Playing at Villa Park is nothing new to Yannick Bolasie, the 29-year-old winger having previously been in the Crystal Palace line-up against Villa.

But he admits he was blown away when he visited our magnificent arena before completing his loan signing from Everton in August.

"When I looked around, I thought WOW!" he said. "I've played at Villa Park, but as a visiting player you just go out on the pitch and don't really take in the surroundings.

"But it was only when I sat in the stand that I realised what a special place it is. I watched the game against Brentford before I signed, and the atmosphere was great."

Yannick, a Democratic Republic of Congo international, is hoping for a repeat of his achievement with Palace in the 2012-13 season, when he helped the London club to promotion.

And his advice to Villa supporters is not to get too disheartened even if the team hit a rough patch.

"Palace were bottom of the table after a few games," he said. "But we went on a run and were promoted via the play-offs."

AUTOGRAPH

FIRST
GOALS
CLUB

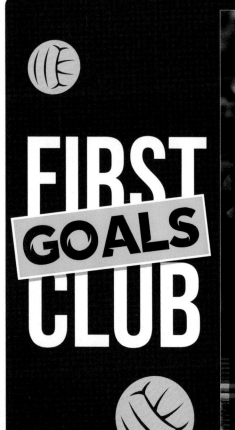

ANDRE GREEN
NORWICH CITY (H) | 19 AUG | 4-2

Keinan Davis headed the ball on to Henri Lansbury three minutes before the interval and the midfielder laid it off for Green to curl a fine right-foot shot into the top corner.

BIRKIR BJARNASON
WIGAN ATHLETIC (H) | 22 AUG | 4-1

With Villa already cruising towards the third round of the League Cup, the Icelandic midfielder had the luxury of stroking home a low shot following Ritchie De Laet's 74th-minute cross from the right.

JOHN TERRY
FULHAM (H) | 21 OCT | 2-1

The former England international times his run to perfection to meet Conor Hourihane's free-kick and plant a firm header inside the near post to put Villa ahead against the Cottagers.

CHRIS SAMBA
SHEFFIELD WED (H) | 4 NOV | 1-2

The towering central defender, on as a substitute for the injured John Terry, is on target from close range in the sixth minute of stoppage time following Callum O'Hare's low cross from the right.

HENRI LANSBURY
LEEDS UTD (A) | 1 NOV | 1-1

With 20 minutes remaining at Elland Road, substitute Lansbury collects a loose ball 30 yards out and moves to the edge of the penalty area before drilling home a powerful right-foot shot to earn a valuable point.

JOSH ONOMAH
BRISTOL CITY (A) | 25 AUG | 1-1

The on-loan Tottenham midfielder latches on to a clearance and smashes it towards goal. The ball takes a deflection off defender Marlon Pack before looping over keeper Frank Fielding and into the net.

KEINAN DAVIS
BARNSLEY (A) | 16 SEPT | 3-0

After Albert Adomah has given Villa a two-goal interval lead, Davis seals an impressive win at Oakwell with a downward header from Ahmed Elmohamady's right-wing cross.

ROBERT SNODGRASS
BURTON ALBION (A) | 26 SEPT | 4-0

With Villa leading 2-0 through Keinan Davis and Albert Adomah, the Scottish winger put the game out of Burton's reach with a left-foot half-volley from just outside the penalty area.

MILE JEDINAK
SHEFFIELD UTD (H) | 23 DEC | 2-2

With Villa already ahead through Albert Adomah's penalty, Jedinak doubles the lead in the ninth minute when he climbs to meet a cross from Robert Snodgrass with a fine header inside the near post.

LEWIS GRABBAN
PRESTON NORTH END (H) | 20 FEB | 1-1

Grabban, on loan from Bournemouth, calmly sends keeper Declan Rudd the wrong way from the penalty spot to earn Villa a point after Keinan Davis is fouled in the area.

GLENN WHELAN
SHEFFIELD WED (A) | 24 FEB | 4-2

The experienced midfielder heads in, close range, from a Robert Snodgrass cross to bring Villa level for the second time. Villa go on to clinch three points with a Conor Hourihane drive and a Robert Snodgrass penalty.

LET'S GO TO THE MOVIES...

Lights, camera, action! Can you guess the Villa players' favourite films?:

To get you started, we can reveal that the third answer is **3C -** James Chester's favourite film is Lock, Stock and Two Smoking Barrels.

1

2

3

4

5

6

7

8

9

A SHAWSHANK REDEMPTION

B THE GREAT ESCAPE

C LOCK, STOCK AND TWO SMOKING BARRELS

D THE BLIND SIDE

E GLADIATOR

F DANCES WITH WOLVES

G INSIDE MAN

I MEET THE PARENTS

J ANY GIVEN SUNDAY

Answers on page 60

A Dresden double...

Villa took a trip down Memory Lane for their final pre-season game ahead of the 2018-19 campaign.

The boys in claret and blue headed for Germany to take on Dynamo Dresden. And just as the Class of 1992 had done, they recorded an excellent victory.

Twenty-six years earlier, Ron Atkinson's men had beaten Dresden 3-1 with goals from Paul McGrath, Tony Daley and Dalian Atkinson.

That match was played at a small non-league ground, but this time the action took place in Dresden's impressive stadium – and once again Villa came out on top.

The home side led at the interval but Andre Green equalised with an unstoppable shot, quickly followed by a fine header which secured a 2-1 success.

Pre-season results mean nothing, of course. These games are intended merely to build the players' match fitness in preparation for competitive action.

But after the 1992 win in Dresden, Villa went on to finish runners-up in the newly-formed Premier League. There will be no complaints if we occupy the same position in the Championship at the end of the season...

2018/19 SQUAD

GK

ØRJAN NYLAND

D.O.B.	BIRTHPLACE
10.09.90	VOLDA

DATE SIGNED	PREVIOUS CLUB
AUG '18	INGOLSTADT

GK

MATIJA SARKIC

D.O.B.	BIRTHPLACE
23.07.97	GRIMSBY

DATE SIGNED	PREVIOUS CLUB
N/A	N/A

GK

MARK BUNN

D.O.B.	BIRTHPLACE
16.11.84	LONDON

DATE SIGNED	PREVIOUS CLUB
JULY '15	NORWICH

GK

ANDRE MOREIRA

D.O.B.	BIRTHPLACE
02.12.95	RIBEIRAO

DATE SIGNED	PREVIOUS CLUB
AUG '18	AT. MADRID

DF

JAMES BREE

D.O.B.	BIRTHPLACE
11.12.97	WAKEFIELD
DATE SIGNED	PREVIOUS CLUB
JAN '17	BARNSLEY

DF

JAMES CHESTER

D.O.B.	BIRTHPLACE
23.01.89	WARRINGTON
DATE SIGNED	PREVIOUS CLUB
AUG '16	WBA

DF

TOMMY ELPHICK

D.O.B.	BIRTHPLACE
07.09.87	BRIGHTON
DATE SIGNED	PREVIOUS CLUB
JUNE '16	B'MOUTH

DF

NEIL TAYLOR

D.O.B.	BIRTHPLACE
07.02.89	ST ASAPH
DATE SIGNED	PREVIOUS CLUB
JAN '17	SWANSEA

DF

RITCHIE DE LAET

D.O.B.	BIRTHPLACE
28.11.88	ANTWERP
DATE SIGNED	PREVIOUS CLUB
AUG '16	LEICESTER

DF

AHMED ELMOHAMADY

D.O.B.	BIRTHPLACE
09.09.87	BASYOUN
DATE SIGNED	PREVIOUS CLUB
JULY '17	HULL CITY

18/19 Squad

17

DF

MICAH RICHARDS

D.O.B.	BIRTHPLACE
24.06.88	BIRMINGHAM

DATE SIGNED	PREVIOUS CLUB
JUNE '15	MAN. CITY

DF

AXEL TUANZEBE

D.O.B.	BIRTHPLACE
14.11.97	BUNIA,CONGO

DATE SIGNED	PREVIOUS CLUB
AUG '18	MAN. UTD

DF

ALAN HUTTON

D.O.B.	BIRTHPLACE
30.11.84	GLASGOW

DATE SIGNED	PREVIOUS CLUB
AUG '11	SPURS

MD

HENRI LANSBURY

D.O.B.	BIRTHPLACE
12.10.90	LONDON

DATE SIGNED	PREVIOUS CLUB
JAN '17	N.FOREST

MD

GLENN WHELAN

D.O.B.	BIRTHPLACE
13.01.84	DUBLIN

DATE SIGNED	PREVIOUS CLUB
JULY '17	STOKE

MD

MILE JEDINAK

D.O.B.	BIRTHPLACE
03.08.84	SYDNEY

DATE SIGNED	PREVIOUS CLUB
AUG '16	C.PALACE

MD · ANDRE GREEN

D.O.B.	BIRTHPLACE
26.07.98	**SOLIHULL**
DATE SIGNED	PREVIOUS CLUB
N/A	**N/A**

MD · CALLUM O'HARE

D.O.B.	BIRTHPLACE
01.05.98	**SOLIHULL**
DATE SIGNED	PREVIOUS CLUB
N/A	**N/A**

MD · BIRKIR BJARNASON

D.O.B.	BIRTHPLACE
27.05.88	**AKUREYRI**
DATE SIGNED	PREVIOUS CLUB
JAN '17	**BASEL**

MD · ALBERT ADOMAH

D.O.B.	BIRTHPLACE
13.12.87	**LONDON**
DATE SIGNED	PREVIOUS CLUB
AUG '16	**M'BORO**

MD · CONOR HOURIHANE

D.O.B.	BIRTHPLACE
02.02.91	**CORK**
DATE SIGNED	PREVIOUS CLUB
JAN '17	**BARNSLEY**

MD · JOHN MCGINN

D.O.B.	BIRTHPLACE
18.10.94	**GLASGOW**
DATE SIGNED	PREVIOUS CLUB
AUG '18	**HIBERNIAN**

18/19 Squad

MD

JACK GREALISH

D.O.B.	BIRTHPLACE
10.09.95	BIRMINGHAM
DATE SIGNED	PREVIOUS CLUB
N/A	N/A

MD

YANNICK BOLASIE

D.O.B.	BIRTHPLACE
24.05.89	LYON
DATE SIGNED	PREVIOUS CLUB
AUG '18	EVERTON

MD

JAKE DOYLE-HAYES

D.O.B.	BIRTHPLACE
30.12.98	BALLYJAMESDUFF
DATE SIGNED	PREVIOUS CLUB
N/A	N/A

MD

ANWAR EL GHAZI

D.O.B.	BIRTHPLACE
03.05.95	BARENDRECHT
DATE SIGNED	PREVIOUS CLUB
AUG '18	LILLE

FW

TAMMY ABRAHAM

D.O.B.	BIRTHPLACE
02/10/97	LONDON
DATE SIGNED	PREVIOUS CLUB
AUG '18	CHELSEA

FW

JONATHAN KODJIA

D.O.B.	BIRTHPLACE
22.10.89	**PARIS**

DATE SIGNED	PREVIOUS CLUB
AUG '16	**BRISTOL C.**

FW

R. HEPBURN-MURPHY

D.O.B.	BIRTHPLACE
28.08.98	**BIRMINGHAM**

DATE SIGNED	PREVIOUS CLUB
N/A	**N/A**

FW

ROSS MCCORMACK

D.O.B.	BIRTHPLACE
18.08.86	**GLASGOW**

DATE SIGNED	PREVIOUS CLUB
AUG '16	**FULHAM**

FW

SCOTT HOGAN

D.O.B.	BIRTHPLACE
13.04.92	**SALFORD**

DATE SIGNED	PREVIOUS CLUB
JAN '17	**BRENTFORD**

FW

KEINAN DAVIS

D.O.B.	BIRTHPLACE
13.02.98	**STEVENAGE**

DATE SIGNED	PREVIOUS CLUB
DEC '15	**BIGGLESWADE**

Do you know JAMES CHESTER?

Test your knowledge of Villa's captain...

1. Where was James born?
   - A. Walsall
   - B. Wolverhampton
   - C. Warrington

2. From which club did he join Villa at the start of the 2016-17 season season?
   - A. Hull City
   - B. West Bromwich Albion
   - C. Manchester United

3. For which country does James play international football?
   - A. England
   - B. Wales
   - C. Republic of Ireland

4. James scored his first Villa goal with a header at Villa Park in February 2017. Who did we beat 1-0 that day?
   - A. Derby County
   - B. Barnsley
   - C. Bristol City

5. Against which team did James make his Villa debut?
   - A. Sheffield Wednesday
   - B. Rotherham United
   - C. Brentford

Answers on page 61

JAC
GR
AL
SH

AVFC

AUTOGRAPH

JOHN McGINN

AUTOGRAPH

AVFC

REVIEW

AUGUST

Conor Hourihane's three goals, plus one from Andre Green, secure a 4-2 home victory over Norwich City and helps everyone to forget defeats by Cardiff City and Reading in the previous two games.

Villa had launched the campaign against Hull City with a first-half goal from Gabby Agbonlahor, only for the visitors to leave Villa Park with a point, and the last game of the month also finishes level after John Onomah's deflected shot cancels out Bristol City's lead at Ashton Gate.

In the League Cup, Villa follow up a first-round win on a rainy night in Colchester by thrashing Wigan Athletic at Villa Park.

AUG RESULTS

05 HULL CITY   H   1-1
🔵 Agbonlahor

09 COLCHESTER (LC1) A   2-1
🔵 Hogan, Kent (og)

12 CARDIFF CITY   A   0-3

15 READING   A   1-2
🔵 Hourihane

19 NORWICH CITY   H   4-2
🔵 Hourihane 3, Green

22 WIGAN ATH (LC2)   H   4-1
🔵 Hogan 2, Adomah, Bjarnason

25 BRISTOL CITY   A   1-1
🔵 Onomah

It's 26 years since a Villa midfielder last scored a hat-trick. Conor Hourihane equals David Platt's treble against Tottenham in 1991 to inspire the team's first Championship win of 2017-18.

25

Albert Adomah takes centre stage during a run which sees Villa unbeaten in the Championship.

After having to settle for a point in back-to-back goalless home draws against Brentford and Middlesbrough, Villa then strike a rich vein of form which brings four consecutive league wins.

Adomah scores twice, including a penalty, in a 3-0 success at Barnsley and is also on target in a 2-1 home win over Nottingham Forest and a 4-0 romp away to Burton Albion.

It's also a special time for Keinan Davis and loan signing Robert Snodgrass, who score their first goals against Barnsley and Burton respectively.

And fit-again Jonathan Kodjia rounds off a successful September by netting the winner against Bolton from the penalty spot.

SEPT RESULTS

09 **BRENTFORD**   H   0-0

12 **M'BORO**   H   0-0

16 **BARNSLEY**   A   3-0
Adomah 2, Davis

19 **M'BORO (LC3)**   H   0-2

23 **NOTTINGHAM F.**   H   2-1
Adomah, Hourihane

26 **BURTON ALBION**   A   4-0
Davis, Adomah, Snodgrass, Onomah

30 **BOLTON W.**   H   1-0
Kodjia (pen)

⚫ Terry, Adomah

2017/18 SEASON
REVIEW
OCT

After going eight Championship matches without defeat, Villa's impressive run comes to an end with a 2-0 defeat by Wolves at Molineux, a result which takes the home side to the top of the table.

But the following week Steve Bruce's side are back to winning ways with a hard-earned home victory over Fulham – and John Terry scores his first goal for the club. The central defender meets Conor Hourihane's inswinging free-kick with a firm header inside the near post, and although the visitors draw level, Albert Adomah hits the winner with a low shot following Josh Onomah's cross.

The Second City derby at St. Andrew's ends goalless, although young striker Keinan Davis is unlucky not to break the deadlock after going on as a substitute, his fierce shot crashing off the bar.

It's a bittersweet month for the boys in claret and blue, who win four of their five games but also lose four players to injuries and illness. John Terry suffers a broken metatarsal, Jonathan Kodjia breaks down with an ankle injury, Mile Jedinak damages his shoulder and Scott Hogan undergoes a stomach operation.

Despite those setbacks, though, Villa continue to pile up the points as they climb to fourth place in the Championship table. After a 2-0 win at Preston, there's a big disappointment in the form of a home defeat to Sheffield Wednesday, but Albert Adomah just can't stop scoring as the team then reel off three consecutive wins in the space of eight days.

The Ghana international is on target twice – including a penalty – as Villa beat QPR 2-1 after going behind at Loftus Road, and he follows up with the first goal in a 2-1 midweek victory over Sunderland, with Josh Onomah netting the second.

And two cool finishes from Adomah secure a 2-0 home win over Ipswich Town.

NOV

2017/18 SEASON
REVIEW

NOV RESULTS

01 PRESTON   A   2-0
⚽ Chester, Snodgrass

04 SHEFFIELD WED   H   1-2
⚽ Samba

18 QPR   A   2-1
⚽ Adomah 2 (1 pen)

21 SUNDERLAND   H   2-1
⚽ Adomah, Onomah

25 IPSWICH   H   2-0
⚽ Adomah 2

DEC REVIEW

A superb diving header from Robert Snodgrass ensures that Villa end 2017 on a high note. The midfielder's classy conversion, following a perfect cross from Albert Adomah, clinches a 1-0 victory over Middlesbrough at The Riverside.

Before that important win, unfortunately, it's very much a case of the bleak mid-winter, with Steve Bruce's side finding little joy throughout December.

Henri Lansbury's powerful shot earns a good point in a 1-1 draw against Leeds United at Elland Road, but Villa are held to home draws by both Millwall and Sheffield United. The result against the Blades is particularly frustrating after Villa go two-up inside nine minutes with an Adomah penalty and Mile Jedinak's first goal for the club.

There are also defeats at Derby County and Brentford, despite a Josh Onomah equaliser at Griffin Park.

DEC RESULTS

01	LEEDS UNITED	A	1-1
	Lansbury		
09	MILLWALL	H	0-0
16	DERBY COUNTY	A	0-2
23	SHEFFIELD UTD	H	2-2
	Adomah (pen), Jedinak		
26	BRENTFORD	A	1-2
	Onomah		
30	M'BORO	A	1-0
	Snodgrass		

JAN
2017/18 SEASON
REVIEW

01 BRISTOL CITY   H   5-0
Snodgrass 2, Hogan, Bjarnason, Hourihane

06 P'BORO' (FAC3)   H   1-3
Davis

13 NOTTINGHAM F.   A   1-0
Hogan

20 BARNSLEY   H   3-1
Hogan 2, Hourihane

30 SHEFFIELD UTD   A   1-0
Snodgrass

The new year couldn't be any happier from a claret-and-blue perspective as Villa kick off 2018 with an emphatic 5-0 victory over promotion rivals Bristol City.

Scott Hogan opens the scoring with a looping header before Robert Snodgrass pounces twice to effectively clinch all three points by the hour mark. Further goals from sub Birkir Bjarnason and midfielder Conor Hourihane complete a scintillating five-star show.

Despite the unexpected setback of an FA Cup exit at the hands of Peterborough United, Villa maintain a 100 per cent Championship record throughout January, earning Steve Bruce the divisional manager-of-the-month award.

Scott Hogan's header clinches three points against Nottingham Forest and the striker follows up with two more goals in a 3-1 home victory over Barnsley, taking his haul to four in three games.

And to round off a productive month, Snodgrass curls home a spectacular late winner against Sheffield United at Bramall Lane.

Villa make hard work of beating bottom-of-the-table Burton Albion, but goals from Scott Hogan, Albert Adomah and Jack Grealish – his first of the season – make it six Championship wins in a row.

That's Villa's best sequence since 1989-90, when Graham Taylor's team reeled off seven straight wins on their way to finishing runners-up to Liverpool in the old First Division – and the seven-game sequence is also equalled when Steve Bruce's boys come out on top in the Second City derby.

Watched by a crowd of 41,233 – the biggest attendance of the season so far – Villa dominate the game against the old enemy from across the city. After a goalless first half, Adomah opens the scoring with a low shot from Grealish's superb pass before Conor Hourihane doubles the lead with a dipping volley from outside the penalty area.

A 2-0 setback at Fulham brings the winning run to an end but Villa are soon picking up points again. Lewis Grabban scores his first goal for the club, netting from the penalty spot to earn a home draw against Preston, and the on-loan striker is also on target against Sheffield Wednesday the following Saturday.

His goal brings Villa level at Hillsborough, and although the home side go ahead again, Glenn Whelan heads a second equaliser in the 67th minute. Then, with a draw looking the most likely outcome, Conor Hourihane blasts home an 87th-minute left-footer before Robert Snodgrass makes it 4-2 with a stoppage-time penalty.

2017/18 SEASON
FEB REVIEW

FEB RESULTS

03 BURTON   H   3-2
🔘 Hogan, Adomah, Grealish

11 BIRMINGHAM   H   2-0
🔘 Adomah, Hourihane

17 FULHAM   A   0-2

20 PRESTON   H   1-1
🔘 Grabban (pen)

24 SHEFFIELD WED   A   4-2
🔘 Grabban, Whelan, Hourihane, Snodgrass (pen)

It's a roller-coaster ride for Villa as they soar to amazing highs and then plunge alarmingly – all in the space of a week!

After a comprehensive victory away to struggling Sunderland, the boys in claret and blue produce what is undoubtedly their best performance of the season to totally destroy Championship leaders Wolves.

Albert Adomah's early goal is cancelled out by a Diogo Jota equaliser but Villa pounce twice in five minutes in the second half to effectively seal victory. James Chester stretches to convert a Robert Snodgrass free-kick before Lewis Grabban scores his fourth goal in as many games by turning Adomah's cross inside the near post.

And just when we think it can't possibly get any better, sub Birkir Bjarnason makes it 4-1 with a fine solo effort.

But after scaling the heights, Villa plunge to the depths. Chester's late goal is only a consolation in a shock home defeat by QPR, and that's followed by another set-back at the hands of Bolton Wanderers and a disappointing goalless draw at Hull City.

2017/18 SEASON
MAR REVIEW

MAR RESULTS

06 SUNDERLAND   A   3-0
⚽ Grabban, Chester, Oviedo (og)

10 WOLVES   H   4-1
⚽ Adomah, Chester, Grabban, Bjarnason

13 QPR   H   1-3
⚽ Chester

17 BOLTON W   A   0-1

31 HULL CITY   A   0-0

The final seven games of the regular season produce four Villa wins and and a draw – with Lewis Grabban on target four times to take his goal haul to eight since arriving on loan in January.

Icelandic midfielder Birkir Bjarnason has the distinction of netting Villa's first goal in April, a perfectly struck shot just after half-time which sets up a comfortable 3-0 home win over Reading .

Conor Hourihane and Scott Hogan are also on target in that game, although Villa have to settle for a Jack Grealish effort in a 3-1 defeat at Norwich City the following weekend.

If that one is no more than a consolation, though, Grealish's magnificent late volley clinches a 1-0 Villa Park victory over Cardiff City, and three nights later Grabban's header secures the same result against Leeds United, which guarantees Villa a place in the play-offs.

Grabban also scores twice in a 4-0 romp at Ipswich and then hits a late equaliser to earn a draw against Derby County, a game watched by 41,745 – Villa Park's biggest crowd for nearly three years.

APR RESULTS

03   READING   H   3-0
⚬ Bjarnason, Hourihane, Hogan

07   NORWICH CITY   A   1-3
⚬ Grealish

10 CARDIFF CITY   H   1-0
⚬ Grealish

13 LEEDS UNITED   H   1-0
⚬ Grabban

21 IPSWICH   A   4-0
⚬ Grabban 2, Hourihane, Bjarnason

28 DERBY COUNTY   H   1-1
⚬ Grabban

MAY RESULTS

07   MILLWALL   A   0-1

THE PLAYOFFS

Villa created a piece of club history after the regular Championship season was over. A fourth-place finish meant the boys in claret-and-blue were involved in the play-offs for the first time since the format was introduced 30 years ago.

It was very much a bittersweet experience. The sweetness was provided by a semi-final victory over Middlesbrough, Steve Bruce's team beating the Teessiders 1-0 on aggregate. But the club's first play-off final ended in bitter disappointment.

A 1-0 defeat by Fulham at Wembley Stadium meant that the Cottagers were promoted to the Premier League, along with champions Wolves and second-placed Cardiff City, while Villa were consigned to a third consecutive season in the Championship.

Over 38,000 Villa supporters created a tremendous atmosphere on the west side of Wembley, but Tom Cairney's 23rd-minute goal left everyone with a feeling of despondency.

There was also a special atmosphere at Villa Park for the second leg of the semi-final. That game ended goalless, but Villa progressed to the final thanks to Mile Jedinak's header in the first leg at The Riverside.

PLAYOFF RESULTS

12	MIDDLESBROUGH	A	1-0
	⚽ Jedinak		
15	MIDDLESBROUGH	H	0-0
26	FULHAM	N	0-1

A football club is about much more than just the first team, and Villa's younger players have won numerous honours over the past few years.

They added two more trophies to the Villa Park cabinet last season, the U23s winning the Premier League Cup in a dramatic final at Swansea and then emerging with silverware at the annual Hong Kong Sevens tournament.

They were in impressive form right from the start of the Premier League competition, losing just one of their six group games to progress to the knockout stage, where goals from Kelsey Mooney and Callum O'Hare clinched a 2-0 victory over Blackburn Rovers in the last 16.

Then it was the turn of Rushian Hepburn-Murphy to take centre stage. The striker, who became Villa's youngest Premier League player when he made his debut at Sunderland in 2015, netted both goals in a 2-1 quarter-final success at Middlesbrough, where the tie was settled in extra-time.

And he produced another late show with an extra-time winner in the semi-final at Leicester City, where he was also on target in normal time. Jack Clarke was the other scorer that night in a thrilling 3-2 victory.

And so to the Liberty Stadium for the final, which was decided on penalties after 90 minutes and extra-time had finished goalless.

Clarke netted the decisive kick in the shoot-out after Jordan Lyden, Mooney and Hepburn-Murphy also scored from the spot.

But it wasn't just about the scorers. Goalkeeper Matija Sarkic also played a vital part with two saves which helped Villa to win the shoot-out 4-2.

A few weeks later, they got their hands on another trophy after winning the Hong Kong Soccer Sevens Shield.

After storming through the group stage with three wins, they beat Kashima Antlers in the semi-final before proving too strong for West Ham in the final.

U23'S
2017/18 SEASON
REVIEW

READING (A) | 15 AUG | 1-2

Conor was on target three minutes from the end at the Madejski Stadium but was unable to prevent defeat.

NOTTINGHAM FOREST (H) | 23 SEPT | 2-1

A superb 30-yard free-kick flew just inside the post to clinch victory after Forest had equalised eight minutes earlier.

CONOR'S 11

Conor Hourihane achieved a rare feat in 2017/18 when he became the first Villa midfielder for over a quarter-of-a-century to reach double figures in the scoring charts.

Here's a reminder of Conor's 11 goals.

NORWICH CITY (H) | 19 AUG | 4-2

Villa were ahead in the 22nd minute against the Canaries when Conor converted a low cross from Keinan Davis.

NORWICH CITY (H) | 19 AUG | 4-2

A fierce drive took a deflection past keeper Angus Gunn following Taylor's free-kick and Lansbury's fine pass.

NORWICH CITY (H) | 19 AUG | 4-2

Hat-trick hero! Five minutes from the end, Conor fired home a precise low shot from Elmohamady's cross.

BRISTOL CITY (H) | 01 JAN | 5-0

Conor's fierce right-foot shot rounded off a five-star performance which earned Villa their biggest win of the season.

BARNSLEY (H) | 20 JAN | 3-1

It was sheer poetry as Conor stroked the ball into the bottom corner following some nifty footwork from Grealish.

BIRMINGHAM (H) | 11 FEB | 2-0

A superb dipping volley over keeper David Stockdale after John Terry's long ball had been headed away.

SHEFFIELD WED (A) | 24 FEB | 4-2

Conor fired Villa into the lead for the first time at Hillsborough before Robert Snodgrass added number four.

READING (H) | 03 APR | 3-0

A firm header from a Snodgrass cross for Villa's second goal in a comfortable victory over the Royals.

IPSWICH (A) | 21 APR | 4-0

Lewis Grabban's shot hit a defender and then the post before Conor nudged the rebound over the line.

See if you can spot the 10 differences between these two pictures.

SPOT the DIFFERENCE

Answers on page 60

PLAYERS AND PLACES

Numerous Villa players have shared their names with places throughout the club's history. Here are just a few...

IAN HAMILTON

More commonly known by his nickname Chico, Hamilton spent nearly seven years at Villa Park, helping the club to the Third Division title in 1972 and promotion from the Second Division in 1975, when he was also in the team that won the League Cup, beating Norwich City at Wembley.

HAMILTON

This town in the central lowlands of Scotland is 12 miles south-east of Glasgow, and is probably best known for its football club, Hamilton Academical. Formed in 1874 – the same year as Villa – Hamilton moved to their new ground, New Douglas Park, in 2001.

TONY MORLEY

A skilful, speedy winger, Morley was a key member of the Villa team that won the League Championship in 1980-81 and the European Cup in 1982. His trickery and low cross set up Peter Withe's winning goal against Bayern Munich in Rotterdam.

MORLEY

A small Yorkshire market town located five miles to the south-west of Leeds city centre. Its town hall is a Grade 1 listed building which is sometimes used for courtroom and wedding scenes in the TV soap Emmerdale.

GARETH BARRY

The Premier League's record-appearance maker played 365 of his top-flight games for Villa. An England international, the classy midfielder was Villa's most consistent performer between 1998 and his departure to Manchester City in 2009.

BARRY ISLAND

This seaside resort in South Wales was made famous when it was used as the primary location in the BBC comedy series Gavin & Stacey. Its pleasure beach is hugely popular with holiday-makers.

HARRY HAMPTON

Although Billy Walker is the club's record league scorer, Harry Hampton holds the record for the most goals. He was on target 215 times in top-flight Villa games, and helped the team to FA Cup glory in 1905 and 1913, plus the league title in 1910.

HAMPTON LOADE

If you have a day out on the Severn Valley Railway, this is one of the stations where the steam train will stop on its journey between Kidderminster and Bridgnorth. Enjoy your trip!

10 YEARS OF
HOME
KITS

2009/10

2010/11

2011/12

2012/13

2013/14

2014/15

2015/16

2016/17

2017/18

2018/19

AUTOGRAPH

Would you believe it?

AT THE DOUBLE

When Villa won the double in 1897, they won both the League Championship and FA Cup on the same day! After beating Everton 3-2 in the Cup Final, they learned that Derby County, the only team who could catch them in the title race, had lost to Bury that afternoon.

LEE'S ON-OFF DEBUT

Lee Hendrie neither started nor finished the match when he made his debut in 1995. The midfielder went on as a 33rd-minute sub for the injured Mark Draper against QPR in December 1995 – but was sent off in added time after being shown a second yellow card. It wasn't the happiest of starts for Lee, particularly as Villa lost 1-0.

WHEN CHARLIE MET JOHNNY...

Full-back Charlie Aitken made the first of his club record 660 appearances in Villa's 4-1 win over Sheffield Wednesday on the final day of the 1960-61 campaign – when midfielder Johnny Dixon played the last of his 430 games for the club. So while Charlie and Johnny were in the first team together only once, they made a staggering 1,090 first-team appearances between them.

DALIAN'S THREE IN A ROW

Dalian Atkinson scored Villa's first goal when the FA Premier League got under way in the 1992-93 season – and he was also on target in the following two games. After netting a late equaliser against Ipswich Town on the opening day, the striker also scored our first Premier League home goal in a midweek game against Leeds United, and followed up with another against Southampton at Villa Park. All three games ended as 1-1 draws.

KEEPER IN MIDFIELD!

Goalkeeper Nigel Spink played the last of his 460 games for Villa in the 1995 game at QPR – but not in goal! Spink, best known for his heroics when he went on as a sub in the 1982 European Cup final, made a different kind of substitute appearance at Loftus Road. He went on as a midfielder after Ian Taylor was injured in stoppage time.

AUTOGRAPH

Getting shirty

Someone has made a muddle of the names on the backs of their shirts. See if you can resolve these anagrams to reveal the correct name of each player.

Shirt	Anagram	Answer
1	V SAID	DAVIS
2	HOME MA LADY	ELMOHAMADY
3	DIN JAKE	JEDINAK
4	RE GEN	GREEN
5	RETCHES	CHESTER
6	AH AMDO	ADOMAH
7	JAR ON BANS	BJARNASON
8	AH ORE	O'HARE
9	BURNSLAY	LANSBURY
10	GO HAN	HOGAN
11	U HONE HAIR	HOURIHANE
12	I A DJ OK	KODJIA

Answers on page 61

Fit for a prince...

When you're a future King of England, there isn't much time for football.

But HRH the Duke of Cambridge has a real passion for the game. Not only is he president of the Football Association, he is also an avid Villa supporter.

Prince William's devotion to the claret-and-blue cause came to light when he sat among Villa's supporters at Wembley for the 2000 FA Cup semi-final against Bolton Wanderers.

It was a winning start for our Royal fan – Villa won on penalties after a goalless draw, although he was obviously disappointed when Chelsea beat John Gregory's side 1-0 in the final.

He had decided to support Villa because all his school friends were Manchester United or Chelsea fans, and the following year he requested a pair of claret-and-blue socks when his father Prince Charles visited Villa Park to open the new Trinity Road stand.

More recently, Price William was at Villa Park for a game against Sunderland – another goalless draw – and then had to present Arsenal with the FA Cup when they beat Villa in the 2015 final.

But it was all smiles for Wills when he paid another visit to Villa Park towards the end of last season. Watching from the stand with our former Norwegian striker John Carew, he was fortunate enough to see Jack Grealish score Villa's goal of the season with a spectacular late volley against Cardiff City.

The goal clinched a dramatic 1-0 win – and it was undoubtedly fit for a prince!

THE Scottish Cafu!

Alan Hutton started the 2018-19 season as Villa's longest-serving player. In August, he celebrated his seventh anniversary in claret and blue.

Yet there was a time when the Scotland international must have thought his time at Villa Park would be short-lived.

After signing from Tottenham Hotspur in 2011, he didn't enjoy the best of fortunes in his first few seasons, and was loaned out to Nottingham Forest, Real Mallorca and Bolton Wanderers.

But in recent times his experience and dedication have shone through, and he has become fondly known by Villa fans as "the Scottish Cafu" – after the legendary Brazilian defender.

Many people thought last season would be Hutton's last with Villa but his consistent performances earned him a new one-year contract.

"It's all I really wanted," he said. "There's no other place I wanted to be. I have a special feeling for the club because I've been here such a long time. This club has a massive history and massive support, and I wanted to remain part of it.

"The fans are amazing and they played a huge part in me wanting to stay here. I had so many messages from supporters on Instagram and it gave me shivers when I read some of the things they said."

Alan was as devastated as anyone when Villa missed out on promotion in last season's Championship play-off final.

"I've grown to love the club and that hurt me deeply," he admitted. "But we have to look forward now."

"The fans are amazing and they played a huge part in me wanting to stay here."

47

AUTOGRAPH

It's Villa Park – but not quite as we know it!

A new pitch was laid at the club's famous venue during the summer. But it wasn't just a case of replacing the playing surface.

The project involved hundreds of hours' work, both for contractors and for Villa's grounds staff, starting on the morning after the final match of last season.

Diggers moved into the stadium, and removed 4,000 tons of material to a depth of nearly 3ft. But this didn't go to waste – it was transported to Bodymoor Heath to build new training ground pitches.

The Aston Academy

School exams can be fun – especially when they are about your favourite football team! Grab a piece of paper and a pen, and check out your Villa knowledge...

Current affairs

1. What was Villa's finishing position in the Championship in 2017-18?

2. Who was the team's leading scorer last season?

3. And who scored Villa's goal of the season?

4. Which member of the Royal Family attended the home game against Cardiff City in March?

5. Exactly 30 years after beating Hull City 5-0 on 1st January 1988, Villa were 5-0 winners on New Year's Day 2018. Who did they beat?

History

1. In which year was Aston Villa formed?

2. Which Irishman (pictured right) scored both goals when Villa beat Manchester United in the 1957 FA Cup final?

3. Villa won the inaugural League Cup competition in 1961. Which Yorkshire club did they beat on aggregate in the final?

4. Which striker became the club's record signing when he arrived from Sunderland in 2011?

5. Who is Villa's highest scorer in Premier League games?

Geography

1. Villa have faced two Italian clubs in UEFA competitions. One is Inter Milan. Can you name the other?

2. In which Dutch city did Villa beat Bayern Munich 1-0 to win the European Cup in 1982?

3. In which French city was striker Jonathan Kodjia born?

4. Which country has provided the most opponents for Villa in European competitions?

5. Villa legend Paul McGrath was born in Ealing, London. But which country did he play for?

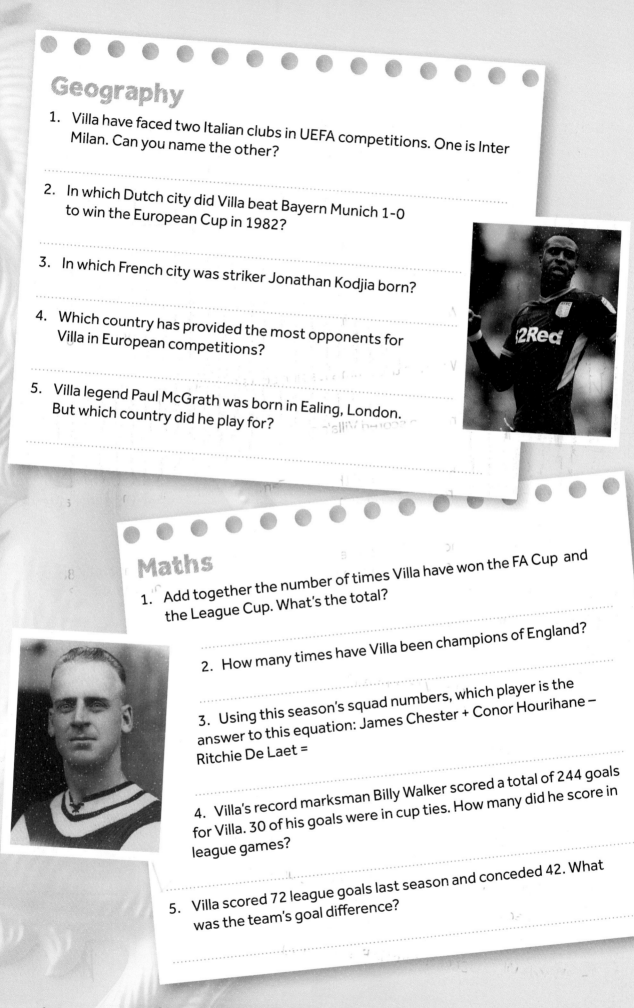

Maths

1. Add together the number of times Villa have won the FA Cup and the League Cup. What's the total?

2. How many times have Villa been champions of England?

3. Using this season's squad numbers, which player is the answer to this equation: James Chester + Conor Hourihane – Ritchie De Laet =

4. Villa's record marksman Billy Walker scored a total of 244 goals for Villa. 30 of his goals were in cup ties. How many did he score in league games?

5. Villa scored 72 league goals last season and conceded 42. What was the team's goal difference?

Answers on page 61

JON
ATH
ON
K
JIA

AVFC

AUTOGRAPH

THAT'S MY HOME!

Villa Park is home for our players, but they come from far and wide. Can you match up these players with their places of birth?

To get you started, we can reveal that the first answer is
1A - James Chester was born in Warrington.

1

A
WARRINGTON

2

B
LONDON

3

C
SYDNEY

4

D
PARIS

5

E
DUBLIN

6

F
GLASGOW

7

G
EGYPT

8

H
SOLIHULL

9

I
ICELAND

10

J
SALFORD

11

K
CORK

12

L
BIRMINGHAM

Answers on page 60

ROAR Lions with the Cubs!

The cubs are ready to roar -- and YOU can roar with them.

Young supporters have always been important to Villa, and that's truer than ever following a major revamp of our junior section.

It started as the Little Villans and then became JV-Life. Now the junior club has been rebranded simply Villa Cubs.

One of Villa's central aims is to welcome families and bring young lions closer to the club – we're very much a Pride of Lions!

That's where Villa Cubs comes in. Membership is FREE to all junior season ticket holders and offers members some great benefits throughout the year. These include:

- A welcome pack, including an exclusive pin badge just for members and a very special backpack that you won't find anywhere else!
- Exclusive competitions.
- The chance to be a flag-bearer.
- Invites to the increasingly-popular Christmas party with the opportunity to meet first-team players.
- A birthday and Christmas card.
- You will also be enrolled into the new Villa Pride Rewards scheme, with loads of competitions offering once-in-a-lifetime prizes.

SO, YOU WANT TO BE A MASCOT?

There are plenty of other opportunities to be closer to the club. Mascots Hercules, Bella and Chip will also be on hand at the many other events held at Villa Park, with a firm focus on welcoming new families.

This is epitomised by the regular Family Fun Zone on match days, an area which continues to grow and improve with the help of supporters' feedback.

And even for those youngsters who are not junior season ticket holders, the cost for all of this is just £20 a year!

To enroll just call 0333 323 1874 or go to www.avfc.co.uk/membership

CONOR
HOURIHANE

AUTOGRAPH

AVFC

THE
NUM3ER5 G4ME

72

Villa have provided 72 players for the England team. Howard Vaughton and Arthur Brown were the first to make their international debuts, scoring five and four goals respectively against Ireland in 1882. Fabian Delph became the latest in the long line of England Villans when he made his debut against Norway in 2014.

1958

Floodlights were installed at Villa Park for the first time in the summer of 1958. They were used for the first time during a 3-2 Monday evening victory over Portsmouth in August that year.

55

Villa Park has hosted 55 FA Cup semi-finals and replays. The first was Tottenham's 4-0 win over West Brom in 1901 and the last was Manchester United's 4-1 success over Watford in 2007.

89

Villa have played a total of 89 games in UEFA competitions – 44 two-leg ties plus the 1982 European Cup final against Bayern Munich.

128

In the 1930-31 season, Villa scored 128 goals when finishing runners-up to Arsenal. The figure remains a record for English football's top flight.

38,141

The number of Villa supporters at Wembley Stadium for last season's Championship play-off final against Fulham.

VITAL
VILLA PARK

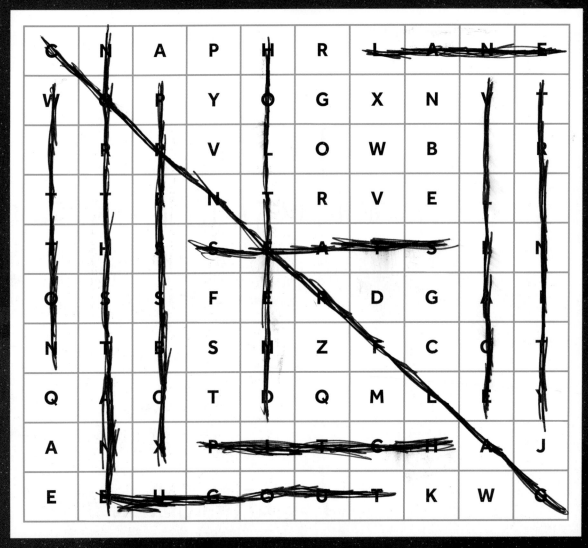

If you're a regular visitor to Villa Park, you should have fun revealing the names of different locations associated with the famous stadium where Villa have played their home matches since 1897.

Some of the words go sideways, some go down and one is diagonal.

Here are the words you are searching for:

HOLTE END	**NORTH STAND**	**PRESS BOX**
TRINITY	**DUG-OUT**	**VILLAGE**
WITTON	**PITCH**	**CORNERFLAG**
LANE	**SEATS**	

Answers on page 61

AUTOGRAPH

LET'S GO TO THE MOVIES...

1F BIRKIR BJARNASON (DANCES WITH WOLVES)

2G ALBERT ADOMAH (INSIDE MAN)

3C JAMES CHESTER (LOCK, STOCK AND TWO SMOKING BARRELS)

4A KEINAN DAVIS (SHAWSHANK REDEMPTION)

5B NEIL TAYLOR (THE GREAT ESCAPE)

6D JAMES BREE (THE BLIND SIDE)

7J ALAN HUTTON (ANY GIVEN SUNDAY)

8E AHMED ELMOHAMADY (GLADIATOR)

9I HENRI LANSBURY (MEET THE PARENTS)

THAT'S MY HOME!

1A JAMES CHESTER (Warrington)

2E GLENN WHELAN (Dublin)

3J SCOTT HOGAN (Salford)

4F ALAN HUTTON (Glasgow)

5K CONOR HOURIHANE (Cork)

6C MILE JEDINAK (Sydney)

7L ANDRE GREEN (Birmingham)

8D JONATHAN KODJIA (Paris)

9H CALLUM O'HARE (Solihull)

10G AHMED ELMOHAMADY (Egypt)

11D ALBERT ADOMAH (London)

12I BIRKIR BJARNASON (Iceland)

SPOT THE DIFFERENCE

Getting shirty

1	DAVIS	7	BJARNASON
2	ELMOHAMADY	8	O'HARE
3	JEDINAK	9	LANSBURY
4	GREEN	10	HOGAN
5	CHESTER	11	HOURIHANE
6	ADOMAH	12	KODJIA

Do you know JAMES CHESTER?

1   C, Warrington
2   B, West Bromwich Albion
3   B, Wales
4   A, Derby County
5   B, Rotherham United

The Aston Academy

Current affairs

1. 4th
2. Albert Adomah
3. Jack Grealish
4. HRH The Duke of Cambridge (Prince William)
5. Bristol City

History

1. 1874
2. Peter McParland
3. Rotherham United
4. Darren Bent
5. Gabby Agbonlahor (74 Premier League goals)

Geography

1. Juventus
2. Rotterdam
3. Paris
4. Spain (5)
5. Republic of Ireland

Maths

1. 12 (7 FA Cup, 5 League Cup)
2. 7
3. 5 + 14 − 2 = 17 Keinan Davis
4. 214
5. 30

VITAL VILLA PARK

CAN YOU SPOT HERCULES IN THE CROWD?